Famous Myths and Legends of the World

Myths and Legends of
SOUTH ASIA
AND
SOUTHEAST ASIA

WORLD
BOOK

a Scott Fetzer company
Chicago
www.worldbook.com

World Book, Inc.
180 North LaSalle Street
Suite 900
Chicago, Illinois 60601
USA

For information about other World Book publications, visit our website at **www.worldbook.com** or call **1-800-967-5325**.

Library of Congress Cataloging-in-Publication Data

Myths and legends of South Asia and Southeast Asia.
    pages cm. -- (Famous myths and legends of the world)
    Summary: "Myths and legends from South and Southeast Asia. Features include information about the history and culture behind the myths, pronunciations, lists of deities, word glossary, further information, and index"-- Provided by publisher.
    Includes index.
    ISBN 978-0-7166-2630-5
    1. Mythology, Indic--Juvenile literature. 2. Hindu mythology--Juvenile literature. 3. Buddhist mythology--Juvenile literature. 4. Mythology, Southeast Asian--Juvenile literature. 5. India--Folklore--Juvenile literature. 6. Southeast Asia--Folklore--Juvenile literature. I. World Book, Inc. II. Series: Famous myths and legends of the world.
    BL1055.M98 2015
    398.20954--dc23
                                        2015014768

Set ISBN: 978-0-7166-2625-1
E-book ISBN: 978-0-7166-2642-8 (EPUB3)

Printed in China by PrintWORKS Global Services, Shenzhen, Guangdong
2nd printing May 2016

Writer: Scott A. Leonard

Staff for World Book, Inc.
Executive Committee
President: Jim O'Rourke
Vice President and Editor in Chief: Paul A. Kobasa
Vice President, Finance: Donald D. Keller
Vice President, Marketing: Jean Lin
Director, International Sales: Kristin Norell
Director, Licensing Sales: Edward Field
Director, Human Resources: Bev Ecker

Editorial
Manager, Annuals/Series Nonfiction: Christine Sullivan
Managing Editor, Annuals/Series Nonfiction:
    Barbara Mayes
Administrative Assistant: Ethel Matthews
Manager, Indexing Services: David Pofelski
Manager, Contracts & Compliance
    (Rights & Permissions): Loranne K. Shields

Manufacturing/Production
Manufacturing Manager: Sandra Johnson
Production/Technology Manager: Anne Fritzinger
Proofreader: Nathalie Strassheim

Graphics and Design
Senior Art Director: Tom Evans
Coordinator, Design Development and Production:
    Brenda Tropinski
Senior Designers: Matthew Carrington,
    Isaiah W. Sheppard, Jr.
Media Researcher: Jeff Heimsath
Manager, Cartographic Services: Wayne K. Pichler
Senior Cartographer: John M. Rejba

Staff for Brown Bear Books Ltd
Managing Editor: Tim Cooke
Editorial Director: Lindsey Lowe
Children's Publisher: Anne O'Daly
Design Manager: Keith Davis
Designer: Mike Davis
Picture Manager: Sophie Mortimer

CONTENTS

MYTHS AND LEGENDS OF
SOUTH ASIA AND SOUTHEAST ASIA

The Hindu god Shiva, armed with a bow and arrows, rides the sacred white bull Nandi. Hindus call Shiva *the Destroyer* because he periodically destroys the world so it can be re-created.

Pictures from History/Bridgeman Images

Note to Readers:

Phonetic pronunciations have been inserted into the myths and legends in this volume to make reading the stories easier and to give the reader some of the flavor of the South Asian and Southeast Asian cultures the stories represent. See page 64 for a pronunciation key.

The myths and legends retold in this volume are written in a creative way to provide an engaging reading experience and approximate the artistry of the originals. Many of these stories were not written down but were recited by storytellers from generation to generation. Even when some of the stories came to be written down they likely did not feature phonetic pronunciations for challenging names and words! We hope the inclusion of this material will improve rather than distract from your experience of the stories.

Some of the figures mentioned in the myths and legends in this volume are described on page 60 in the section "Deities of South Asia and Southeast Asia." In addition, some unusual words in the text are defined in the Glossary on page 62.

INTRODUCTION

Since the earliest times, people have told stories to try to explain the world in which they lived. These stories are known as myths. Myths try to answer such questions as, How was the world created? Who were the first people? Where did the animals come from? Why does the sun rise and set? Why is the land devastated by storms or drought? Today, people often rely on science to answer many of these questions. But in earlier times—and in some parts of the world today—people explained natural events using stories about gods, goddesses, spirits of nature, and heroes.

The World of Krishna, page 32

Myths are different from folk tales and legends. Folk tales are fictional stories about animals or human beings. Most of these tales are not set in any particular time or place, and they begin and end in a certain way. For example, many English folk tales begin with the phrase "Once upon a time" and end with "They lived happily ever after." Legends are set in the real world, in the present or the historical past. Legends distort the truth, but they are based on real people or events.

Myths, in contrast, typically tell of events that have taken place in the remote past. Unlike legends, myths have also played—and often continue to play—an important role in a society's religious life. Although legends may have religious themes, most are not religious in nature. The people of a society may tell folk tales and legends for amusement, without believing them. But they usually consider their myths sacred and completely true.

Most myths concern *divinities* or *deities* (divine beings). These divinities have powers far greater than those of any human being. At the same time, however, many gods, goddesses, and heroes of mythology have human characteristics. They are guided by such emotions as love and jealousy, and they may experience birth and death. A number of mythological figures even look like human beings. In many cases, the human qualities of the divinities reflect a society's ideals. Good gods and goddesses have the qualities a society admires, and evil ones have the qualities it dislikes. In myths, the actions of these divinities influence the world of humans for better or for worse.

The World of Buddhism, page 36

Myths can sometimes seem very strange. They sometimes seem to take place in a world that is both like our world and unlike it. Time can go backward and forward, so it is sometimes difficult to tell in what order events happen. People may be dead and alive at the same time.

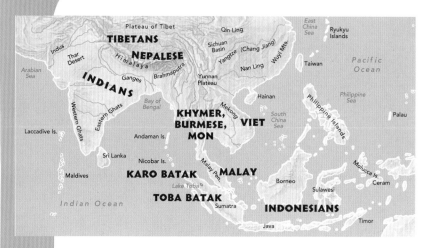

Myths were originally passed down from generation to generation by word of mouth. Partly for this reason, there are often different versions of the same story.

South Asia and Southeast Asia lie at a crossroads between Europe in the west and China and Japan in the east. Their histories were shaped by trade and the exchange of ideas and beliefs.

In early times, every society developed its own myths, though many myths across cultures share similar themes, such as a battle between good and evil. The myths of a society generally reflect the landscape, climate, and society in which the storytellers lived. Myths tell people about their distant history. They show people how to behave in the world and find their way. As teaching tools, myths help to prepare children for adulthood.

Myths of South Asia and Southeast Asia

The Indian subcontinent was the birthplace of three of the world's great religions: Hinduism, Buddhism, and Jainism. The religious beliefs and practices of Hindus vary enormously. Hinduism has many gods, and its myths often tell of their deeds. Hindus also have many sacred texts, including the Vedas and the Upanishads. These writings serve as a guide to moral conduct.

Buddhism, on the other hand, has no gods. Its stories usually take the form of moral tales that show the listener the principles of the Buddhist faith. Jainism is based on the belief that every living thing consists of an eternal soul, called the jiva, and a temporary physical body. The eternal jiva is imprisoned in the body as a result of involvement in worldly activities. To free the jiva, one must avoid such activities as much as possible.

Unlike many mythologies from around the world, the myths of the Hindus, Buddhists, and Jainists are not the relics of a culture that has disappeared. They are part of contemporary religions that play an important role in the lives of millions of worshipers.

The World of the Fairy Queen, page 52

By studying myths, we can learn how different societies have answered basic questions about the world and the individual's place in it. We can learn how a people developed a particular social system with its many customs and ways of life. By examining myths, we can better understand the feelings and values that bind members of society into one group. We can compare the myths of various cultures to discover how these cultures differ and how they resemble one another. We can also study myths to try to understand why people behave as they do.

BRAHMA
Creates the World

The Indian Hindus use this myth to explain the origin of the world and the different classes of people who lived in India. The myth also explains the origins of India's many—but interconnected—deities.

From time to time, the universe dissolves. Everything falls into silence and watery darkness. All things, all beings, and all ideas fall into the great, boundless Oneness of the god Brahma (BRAH muh). In the beginning, Brahma slept upon the waters of nothingness. Who knows how many ages he slept? When he awoke, he wanted to create something. He took the form of a giant boar and dived deep into the watery darkness.

There, Earth woke and prayed to her Lord, begging him to rescue her from the darkness. With his tusks, Brahma carried Earth to the surface of the waters, where she floated like a great boat. Brahma, the Lord of Creation, then divided the land into seven continents. He put the mountains in their proper places.

Brahma has four arms, four faces, and four mouths. From him the four kinds of being arose. The asuras (ah SOO rahz), the demons, came from his thighs. The devas (DAY vahs), the gods of light, arose next, exhaled from Brahma's mouth. The pitris (PIH trees), the ancestors, rushed from Brahma's sides, filling the world.

Finally, came the humans. Brahma produced four kinds of humans. The Brahmans (BRAH muhnz)—religious leaders and scholars—emerged from the Creator's mouth. The Kshatriyas (KSHAT ree yuhz)—rulers, nobles, and warriors—came from his arms. The Vaisyas (VYS yuhz)—farmers, landowners, traders, and moneylenders—flowed from his thighs. And last, through Brahma's feet, came the Shudras (SHOO druhz)—artists and laborers.

Who can sing all the wonders Brahma created from his divine body? From his mouths came speech, which allowed people to reveal their thoughts and hear the thoughts of others. From Brahma's unknowable mind flowed the Vedas, the sacred books, bringing history and guidance. From his tongue flowed amrita, the milk of life that animates all living things. From his nose, the stars and sky took shape, providing signposts for travelers and a canopy for all living things. The sun and heavens emerged from the pupils of his eyes to warm and watch over us. His ears produced places of worship so there might be dignity and places to honor the gods. Clouds and rain flowed from his hair to water and nourish the soil.

When all things had again been assigned their proper place, Brahma the Creator assumed the form of Vishnu (VIHSH noo) the Preserver. Lord Vishnu, like the roots of a mighty tree, supports, nourishes, and preserves all. He governs the universe and is the inward

nature of every element within it. And so it shall be until Vishnu transforms into Shiva (SHEE vuh) the Destroyer, who will bring fire to devour the universe. Then all things will again fall into silence and a watery darkness upon which Brahma will sleep.

The World of INDIA

The huge number of gods and beliefs in India arises from that country's complex history of people *migrating* (moving) from one area to another. Original settlers to what is now India were probably related to the people who became Aboriginal Australians. Later waves of invaders from the Middle East and Central Asia followed. Invaders collectively called the Aryans (meaning *nobles*) arrived around 1800 B.C. Aryan worship emphasized many of the rituals that characterize modern Indian religious devotion.

MYTH AND RELIGION

Unlike many other collections of myths, Hindu myths come from a religious tradition that is still practiced. There are about one billion Hindus in the world. Most of them live in India, where they are the majority of the population. Hinduism has no central authority, so it may vary among its followers. It has many sacred texts rather than just one, as with the Bible or the Koran, and many gods. Hindus can choose whether to worship one or many gods.

Followers of the Hindu sky god Indra in Kathmandu, Nepal, celebrate during a festival held each fall to mark the end of the windy and rainy monsoon season. A warlike god, Indra resembles the ancient Greek god Zeus. Both the ancient Greeks and the ancient people of India descended from a common culture called the Indo-European community.

Young Hindu students recite verses from the Vedas at a monastery in Tamil Nadu, India. The Vedas are the oldest sacred texts of Hinduism. They were probably composed beginning about 1400 B.C.

A Hindu priest performs a ritual called a fire puja along the banks of the Ganges River in India. During puja, people light wicks soaked in *ghee* (purified butter) or camphor, a product of the camphor tree. The sweet-smelling smoke is offered as a gift to the gods.

A Hindu statue represents the Trimurti (trih MUR tee), the three forms of Brahman (BRAH muhn), the name of the most absolute, abstract form of God in the Hindu religion. The forms are Brahma (BRAH muh) the Creator, Vishnu (VIHSH noo) the Preserver, and Shiva (SHEE vuh) the Destroyer.

THE CREATION

For the Tibetans, this myth explains the creation of the world and why their lives in the mountains became so difficult after the gods became humans.

In the beginning, a breeze stirred the emptiness. After years without number, the wind thickened into Dorje Gyatram (DAWR juh GY uh tram), the Mighty Double Thunderbolt. Dorje Gyatram formed clouds, which poured rain for uncountable years, creating a vast ocean. All was quiet, and the endless sea grew as clear as glass.

Then once again, the winds began to stir, whipping up foam on the water like butter in a churn. After uncountable years, Earth rose like a mountain from the foam. And still the wind blew, rushing between mountain peaks and

sweeping water droplets into clouds from which torrents fell, making Earth's oceans, lakes, and rivers.

Sumeru, the mountain at the center of the universe, is home to the gods and their children. Surrounding Sumeru are seven lakes separated by seven mountain ranges. Riding on the waters of the outermost lake are the four worlds, each with its own nature and its own inhabitants. Our world, Dzambu Ling (zam boo lihng), is in the south. In olden times, the gods from Sumeru lived here. There was no pain, sickness, or want.

OF THE WORLD

One day, one of the gods noticed a large pot containing a creamy substance. He tasted it and found it delicious. Soon the gods were eating it as often as they could. But as they ate, their powers and the light beaming from their bodies faded. The once-mighty gods became the first humans. In the sky, the sun, moon, and stars appeared.

When the creamy substance was gone, the first men took to eating the fruit of the nyugu (nyoo goo) plant. Each day, the plant bore one fruit. But one day, one man discovered that his nyugu plant had borne two fruits. He ate both. But

the next day, his plant had no fruits at all. So he stole a fruit from his neighbor. That neighbor, now having no fruit of his own, stole fruit from his neighbor, and on it went. People now knew greed, theft, and fear. One day, a man felt such terrible pain in the parts that made him a man that he tore them off and became a woman. The woman had children, who grew up and had children of their own. The world came to know suffering, disease, aging, and death.

The people grew so miserable that they appointed a king to organize them. He showed them how to live in peace, giving each person land on which to build shelter and grow food. So when we feel the warmth of the sun and see the moon and stars, we are reminded that, if not for our ancestors, we would live in darkness. And if not for the greed of one person, the world would not know suffering.

The World of
THE TIBETANS

Tibet, which today is a part of China, is a land in south-central Asia. It is often called the *Roof of the World* because its snow-covered mountains and windswept plateau are the highest in the world. The world's highest mountain, Mount Everest, rises in southern Tibet. Tibetan Buddhism has practices and beliefs distinct from other forms of Buddhism.

SACRED MOUNTAINS

Sacred mountains appear in many mythic traditions. Tibetans *venerate* (worship) mountain deities believed to inhabit various peaks. The Bon tradition, which is older than Buddhism in Tibet, venerates nine mountains as the homes of powerful gods. Four religions—Buddhism, Hinduism, Bon, and Jainism—consider Mount Kailash in Tibet as sacred and associate it with divinities central to their belief systems.

↑
A Tibetan *shaman* (holy man) beats a drum during a religious ritual. In traditional Tibetan religion, shamans link the people to the spirit world.

Tibetan Buddhists walk around the base of Mount Kailash in Tibet. Thousands of pilgrims make the 32-mile (52-kilometer) journey around the mountain each year.

Mythologies around the world feature "Golden Age" stories. These stories recall a time in the distant past when people lived in harmony and did not suffer from death, aging, and disease. Some event, however, always causes these ideal conditions to change into the difficult world in which we actually live.

A Tibetan woman lights candles in the Ramoche Temple in Lhasa as offerings to an image of Buddha. The candles represent the light of wisdom illuminating the darkness of ignorance.

Ganden Monastery, a Buddhist monastery, clings to the side of Wangbur Mountain, near Lhasa, Tibet. It dates from the early 1400's. Religion is extremely important in Tibet. In the past, large numbers of Tibetan men became monks, and a smaller number of women became nuns. Every town and valley had a *monastery* (a home to monks) or *convent* (a home to nuns), and some had several.

The Origins of the Viet

This story reminds the Vietnamese that, whether they were born in the mountains or near the sea, they are all one people.

In ancient times, monsters threatened the people of Linh Nam (lihng nahm). The young dragon god Lac Long Quan (lak long won) defeated the monsters. He taught the people how to build homes, cook, and make clothes—all the things necessary for a good and orderly life. The grateful people built him a palace in the mountains. But Lac Long Quan longed to return to the sea. He left, saying, "If trouble comes, call for me!"

Some time afterward, invaders from the north occupied Linh Nam. The people called Lac Long Quan, who appeared at once. He disguised himself and visited the chief of the northern invaders. There he met a young woman of great beauty. She was Au Co (OW gah), the chief's daughter. It was love at first sight. Lac Long Quan carried his bride to his palace.

Soon after, Au Co gave birth to 100 eggs. Inside each was a boy, who grew into a handsome man. But Lac Long Quan missed the sea. He told Au Co, "It is hard for me, a dragon of the sea, and you, a fairy from the mountains, to live together. I will take 50 of our sons with me to the sea. You take 50 of our sons to the mountains. If either of us is in trouble, we will come to the other's aid."

And so it was. Lac Long Quan took 50 sons to the coast and taught them how to fish and to plant and harvest rice. Au Co took 50 sons to the mountains and taught them how to raise livestock and to grow fruit trees. The Vietnamese people believe they descended from the 100 sons of Lac Long Quan and Au Co. To this day, they call themselves the children of the Dragon and the Fairy.

The World of
THE VIET

Archaeological evidence suggests there is some historical truth to the story that an ancient generation of the people of what is now Vietnam parted ways to populate the mountains and the coasts. The early Vietnamese living along the coasts and river deltas founded the Lac kingdom. They became fishers and farmers, developing a sophisticated wet-rice farming system as early as 1500 B.C. Scholars believe other Vietnamese in the mountains protected the coastal Lac from northern invaders in exchange for rice and other crops. Thus the partnership between the Earth people of Au Co (OW gah) and the water people of Lac Long Quan (lak long won) may have historical as well as religious and cultural meaning.

Limestone rocks create strange formations in Ha Long Bay in Vietnam's Gulf of Tonkin. Vietnamese myth says the rocks were formed when a family of dragons sent by the gods to protect the Viet crashed to Earth. Geologists have determined that the Ha Long Bay area initially formed the floor of a prehistoric ocean. Over thousands of years, as water levels rose and fell, the soft limestone gradually eroded into its present shape.

LAND AND SEA

The union between Lac Long Quan and Au Co—and between the sea and the mountains—reflects Vietnam's geography. Vietnam is an S-shaped country that occupies the rugged eastern Indochinese Peninsula. The country is just 31 miles (50 km) across at its widest point, but has a coastline that is 2,025 miles (3,260 kilometers) long. Inland, the country is dominated by hills and mountains covered with rain forest.

Vietnamese farmers walk through terraced fields of rice.

GODS IN DISGUISE

Myths around the world feature gods disguising themselves as humans for various purposes. In the *Iliad*, Homer describes how the Greek gods interfere in the Trojan War. Odin, the Norse father of the gods, was believed to appear as an old man with a staff, cloak, and pointed hat. This disguise may have inspired the appearance of the wizard Gandalf the Grey in *The Hobbit* (1937) and other books by British writer J. R. R. Tolkien.

A Vietnamese fisherman carries his net home at sunset. In Vietnam, which has a long coastline, the sea is a major source of food.

THE NAGA, THE SUN, AND

This Burmese myth explains why the crow has black feathers. But it also explains why the Burmese are poor.

In times past, the Nagas (NAH guhz)—the race of dragons—lived in a lake in the northern mountains of Burma. Once, a Naga princess grew curious about the humans she saw fishing and washing their clothes in her waters. Eventually, she grew so curious that she adopted the beautiful body of a young woman so she could watch the villagers from the rocks along the shore.

The Sun saw the beautiful Naga princess and fell in love with her. Each day, his longing grew. Finally, he took the form of a handsome young hunter and approached her. To his delight, the beautiful young woman returned his love, and they married.

THE CROW

Soon, the Sun began neglecting his duties. He rose late and left the sky early to be with his bride. People complained. At last, the Sun could no longer ignore them. "My love," he said. "I must return to the sky." The Naga princess wept and gently touched her belly, inside which her and the Sun's child was growing.

The Sun kissed her and then called his helper, White Crow. This bird was extremely proud of his feathers, which shone brilliantly in the light. The Sun said, "When our children are born, my crow will bring me the good news."

The princess was lonely without the Sun, so she returned to her watery realm. Days passed. Then months. But at long last, the princess left the lake and gave birth to three beautiful eggs. She sent White Crow to tell her husband. The Sun was overjoyed with the news. He found a huge ruby and put it in a silk bag. "Take this to the princess so she can buy a kingdom for our children to rule over," he told White Crow. "They will want for nothing!" "I will! I will!" White Crow cawed and flew off. But by the

time he reached Earth, White Crow was tired. The silk bag was so heavy. Then he smelled food. "A festival!" he cried. "I can stop to refresh myself."

White Crow hung the silk bag in a tree, and hopped away to steal some food. He did not see that a merchant was watching. The man knew birds are messengers of the spirit world. He opened the bag and put the ruby in his pocket. To hide his theft, the man put some dung and stones in the silk bag.

At sundown White Crow remembered his errand, picked up the bag, and flew to the princess. She was warming her eggs by the side of the lake. "For you! For you!" said White Crow.

The princess's joy at receiving the gift turned to fury when she opened the bag. She had been insulted! Without a word, she slipped beneath the waves, leaving her eggs on the shore. The Sun was furious when he learned of White Crow's carelessness. He punished the bird by burning his feathers black. That is why all crows now have black feathers.

The World of THE NAGA

Burma is also known as Myanmar (myahn MAHR). The first known people to live in what is now Myanmar were the Mon. They moved into the Myanmar region as early as 3000 B.C. Other peoples who later migrated to the area include the Pyu, Burmans, Chin, Kachin, Karen, and Shan.

Most crows are black. Some species have white in their plumage, but all-white crows are unusual.

The Mon people of Burma, the Angkor dynasty who ruled Cambodia, and the Viet of Vietnam have traditionally believed that they were descended from Nagas, who lived in the deep waters of mountain lakes or in the oceans.

MYTHS AND BIRDS

Because birds are creatures of Earth and sky, they play an important role in many myths. In ancient Greece and Rome, birds were believed to deliver *omens* (signs of things to come). Crows accompanied the Norse god Odin. In the myths of many Native American and Pacific Island nations, birds carry messages between our world and the spirit world. Hawks and eagles, which see widely as they soar for long periods, are associated with wisdom.

Burma is famous for the flawless deep red color and clarity of its rubies. The precious stones have been mined there for thousands of years. In the past, Burmese warriors cut themselves to insert rubies beneath their skin as a form of magical protection in battle.

In Asian *lore* (stories), dragons represent the forces of change and renewal, luck and protection. The Sanskrit word for dragon is *naga*, originally referring to a snake having many heads. *Naga* can also mean *spring* (a time of renewal). The story about the Naga princess embodies these ideas: The Sun shirks his duties for his new wife, and the world becomes colder and darker as it does in winter. When the Sun returns to his duties, the Naga princess's eggs are born (a sign of rebirth).

Colorfully costumed dancers from the Naga culture of northwestern Burma perform a traditional dance. Such dances are usually presented at festivals and religious events. The dancers are accompanied by trumpets, drums made of cattle hides or logs, and mouth organs and flutes made of bamboo.

INDRA DEFEATS

This Hindu myth helps to explain the power of Indra and how the god can protect humans from drought and other natural disasters.

VRITRA

Indra, the Lord of Gods, possessed great strength and many weapons. It was his custom to gather the devas (DAY vahs), the gods of light, to make war on the asuras (ah SOO rahz), the demons of the dark. Indra and his army overcame the demons every time. Yet it troubled Indra that, despite so many defeats, the asuras remained powerful.

At last, Indra discovered that the demons got their strength from the powerful prayers of a sage. Indra, the God of War, was consumed with anger and struck the head of this holy man from his shoulders.

But the sage's father mourned his son's death. Craving vengeance, the father created the mighty demon Vritra (VRIHT ruh). This asura had the body of a dragon; cruel fangs and claws; hard, coppery scales; and a tail thicker than the mightiest tree. Vritra was selfish and cruel, and in his greed, he drank all the waters of Earth. Soon the living things on Earth began to perish.

Then Vritra, the Firstborn of Dragons, challenged Indra. Indra fought valiantly, but he was defeated and imprisoned by Vritra. Vishnu (VIHSH noo) the Preserver begged Vritra to release Indra. Vritra agreed. "But," hissed Vritra, "the Leader of Devassss must never raise weaponsssss of wood, sssstone, or metal againsssssst me again. He may not wield anything wet or dry. He may not attack during night or day!"

Indra agreed, but inwardly he longed to destroy the demon and release the life-giving waters. So Indra befriended Vritra, the Firstborn of Dragons, hoping to discover a secret weakness. "I have been given power so that I may not be killed at night or during the day," boasted Vritra. Yes, thought Indra, but evening is neither night nor day. But how could he attack the demon without a weapon? Indra and the devas decided the only weapon he could use must be made from the bones of a holy man.

But who would make such a sacrifice?

Indra and the devas approached the sage Dadhichi (DUH hee chee) and explained their awful plan. To their surprise, the great sage agreed to give them his bones. "Better my bones should serve the cause of good than rot in the ground," he said. And so the devas took Dadhichi's bones and fashioned the Great Thunderbolt, Indra's most fearsome weapon.

Indra prepared himself for war. He drank a great quantity of soma, the sacred drink that gives immortality and divine energy. Strengthened, the Lord of Gods swept down from heaven one evening in a golden chariot to the mountain around which Vritra slept in a coil.

"Vritra!" bellowed Indra, "I command you to release the waters that give life to Earth and the gods!"

"Who wakessss me from ssssleep?" demanded Vritra.

"It is Indra, the Storm Lord, owner of the heavens! Release the waters or I will bring my fury against you!"

"Fool!" snarled Vritra, "Do you not know I am Firstborn of Dragonssss, King of the Demon Hosssst?! All fear me! I will never releasssse the waterssss!"

Spreading his fearsome wings, Vritra leapt into the sky, aiming his claws at Indra. The Lord of Gods dodged this assault, but the battle raged on. The god and demon exchanged many blows, but neither managed to inflict more than a few cuts and bruises on the other. Soon, all the gods and demons had assembled, each faction cheering its champion.

At last, Indra stretched far above the clouds and grasped the Great Thunderbolt. Seeing that his enemy was exposed, Vritra sprang at the Storm Lord, with his fangs bared and his claws out. But Indra hurled the Great Thunderbolt at Vritra, striking the demon in the belly and ripping him open. At that moment, all the water within him fell to Earth, refilling lakes, rivers, and wells.

The mighty demon toppled from the sky, his lifeless body crashing to the ground. This is how Indra freed Earth from drought. And that is why the Storm Lord is also known as the Slayer of Vritra.

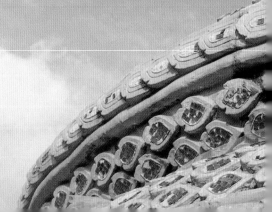

The World of INDRA

Hinduism is India's most widespread religion and the world's third-largest faith. It has no single founder or philosophy but brings together many different traditions, regional cults, and philosophical viewpoints. Among its root traditions is the ancient religion of the Vedas, the oldest Hindu scriptures, which stress the importance of ritual, ethics, and *mantras* (devotional chanting). Various mystical traditions within Hinduism emphasize meditation and the effort to achieve *moksha* (Enlightenment) by casting off desire and living a life of simplicity and compassion.

Women carry pots of water on their heads as they cross an arid region of Rajasthan, India, during a dry season. Droughts like the one described in "Indra Defeats Vritra" have killed tens of millions of people in India over the centuries. Much of the country depends on favorable monsoon winds in the summer to bring rain. If the monsoon fails, crops fail and hunger may follow.

A Hindu *sadhu* (holy man) in traditional clothing sits on the *ghats* (stairways) to the holy Ganges River in the Indian city of Varanasi.

HINDU GODS

Hindus believe that Indra was a *demigod* (lesser god) who was created by Brahma (BRAH muh). Brahma himself was said to have been born from the navel of Vishnu (VIHSH noo), one of the three greatest gods. Brahma put each demigod in charge of a part of the universe. Indra controlled the rain. Vayu was in charge of the wind; Surya, the sun; and Chandra, the moon. The goddess Bhumi controlled Earth, and Varuna was in charge of the oceans and rivers.

THE VEDAS

The Vedas are a large body of writings believed to have been dictated by Brahma, the Creator, part of the Hindu Trimurti (trinity). The Vedas are divided into four collections. One of them, called the Rigveda, contains hymns from which stories like "Indra Defeats Vritra" come. The other three collections outline the requirements for rituals and sacrifices and contain the mantras used in religious ceremonies.

People throw colored powder and spray water over one another during Holi (HOH lee), a popular Hindu festival associated with the god Vishnu, springtime, and the grain harvest. The liveliness of Holi commemorates the playful character of the god Krishna as a boy. Holi gets its name from a story in the *Puranas*, a collection of myths about Hindu gods and goddesses and heroes. In the story, Vishnu protects a prince from a demon goddess.

The Killing of the
DEMON

Hindus show the power of Krishna, one of their most important gods, by telling of how he overcame a demon in the shape of a giant snake.

One morning, the Lord God Krishna (KRIHSH nuh) decided to go for a picnic in the forest with his friends the gopas, the cowherd boys. Despite his great power, Krishna appears to most people as a beautiful boy-child. And so he seemed to his friends.

Blowing his buffalo-horn trumpet, Krishna called the gopas and their herds. The boys' mothers sent them off arrayed in red beads, golden ornaments, and festive flowers. Such is the joy in Krishna's presence that the boys further adorned themselves with peacock feathers and with powders made of colorful minerals, fruit, and leaves.

The gopas were in high spirits. They played their flutes and horns, made silly faces, and teased one another. All the forest animals joined the boys in their play. But just out of sight crawled the demon Aghasura (ah gas soor uh). His eyes burned with hatred, for he

had a grudge against Krishna. "This boy slew my brother and sister," raged the demon. "I will offer his life to my siblings so they may know peace."

Using his great powers, Aghasura turned himself into a snake as long as a river and as tall as a hill. He lay on the forest

AGHASURA

floor, opened his mouth wide and waited.

When the gopas came to Aghasura's mouth, they mistook it for a cave and ran inside. The demon waited, hoping Krishna would follow his friends. At last the god entered Aghasura's mouth. SNAP! The mighty jaws closed.

The gopas fainted from fear. But Krishna remained calm. Lodged in the demon's throat, the god changed shape. He expanded into a stone that blocked the demon's throat. Choking, Aghasura thrashed wildly, his eyes bulging from their sockets. Finally, with a mighty BOOM, the wind pent up in the demon's lungs exploded through the top of his skull, and he died.

Krishna revived his friends and led them from the snake's jaws. The gods rejoiced at the slaying of the demon. Flowers rained upon Krishna as he and the gopas continued on their way, laughing.

31

The World of KRISHNA

Krishna (KRIHSH nuh) is one of the most popular Hindu gods, worshiped throughout India. He is often shown as a blue-skinned boy playing a flute. The blue color represents his association with the blue lotus, a sacred flower in India. Krishna is also portrayed as a youthful prince with his *consort* (companion), the milkmaid Radha, standing at his side. Hindus consider Krishna to be the eighth *avatar* (physical form) of the god Vishnu (VIHSH noo) the Preserver. They believe Krishna was born to rid the world of evil and to give delight to his many friends and lovers.

SNAKES IN INDIA

The people who heard the story of Aghasura (ah gas soor uh) turning into a giant snake would have been very familiar with snakes. India is home to some of the most poisonous snake species. Hindus see some snakes as destroyers but also as protectors. Snakes are important symbols in Indian mythology. The creator god Vishnu sleeps on a seven-headed serpent named Shesha. Shiva the Destroyer is usually portrayed with a cobra around his neck.

The king cobra is one of the most dangerous snakes in India. It can stand up to one-third of its 18-foot (5.5-meter) adult length to attack.

Shape-shifting, or changing one's appearance, occurs in many myths. Some figures change form for protection or to gain an advantage. Other figures are changed as punishment. The Greek god Zeus changes into a swan, a bull, and even a golden rain shower in his pursuit of women. Loki, the Norse trickster, changes shape to work mischief. The transformations usually involve changing from a human to an animal but may also involve changing into a plant or an *inanimate* (nonliving) object.

Krishna was not the only Hindu god who could change shape. In one of his avatars, Vishnu the Preserver took the form of a fish, Matsya. In this form, Vishnu was said to have saved humans from a huge flood long ago. Matsya is portrayed as a fish or as a fish with a human torso and the four arms of Vishnu.

THE GOAT
Who Saved the Priest

For Buddhists in Southeast Asia, this myth explains the nature of being reborn and why killing and sacrificing animals is wrong.

In ancient times, a priest of an old religion asked his followers to prepare a goat for sacrifice. He thought it would please his god. The followers took the goat to the river to bathe it and adorn it with flowers.

The goat realized he was about to die, and his past lives flashed through his mind. He understood that with this death, he would be free from the karma he had accumulated from his bad actions in his previous lives. He would be free to move on to another existence! So the goat laughed a loud goat-laugh. But the goat also realized that the priest would collect bad karma by conducting this sacrifice. The priest would suffer many lives and unpleasant deaths for committing this ignorant act. And so the goat cried a terrible goat-cry.

The priest's followers were amazed and asked, "Sir goat, why did you laugh loudly and then cry just as loudly?" "I will tell you," said the goat, "but only if your master hears my explanation."

So they brought the goat to the priest and told him what had happened. "My friend," the goat said, "a long time ago, I was a priest like you. In my ignorance, I too sacrificed animals to my gods. And because of my actions, my karma required that I should be beheaded in my next 499 lives!

Today, I realized that with my 500th death, my past misdeeds will no longer have power over me. I will be free. And so I laughed. But I also realized that, by sacrificing me, you would be doomed to have your head chopped off in your next

500 lifetimes. Out of compassion for your future suffering, I wept."

The priest said, "Well, sir goat, I will not kill you. What is more, I will do all in my power to protect you from harm."
"That is kind," said the goat. "But your power is weak compared with karma. The consequences of my misdeeds will be accomplished no matter what."

So the priest released the goat. He and his followers surrounded the animal, ready to prevent any harm from coming to him. The goat wandered to the foot of the mountains to nibble some leaves. Suddenly, a lightning bolt struck the rocks above, breaking off a sharp stone that hurtled down and beheaded the goat.

Hearing of this event, hundreds of people gathered. A tree-spirit appeared in the air above them. "Do you see what happened to this goat?" asked the spirit. "All beings are born, live, age, and die. Each being wishes to live happily. But, ignoring this common bond, some kill other living beings. This causes suffering, now and in countless rebirths. Every deed produces consequences. Killing and misdeeds heap up suffering for those who do them. Each time you kill, part of you dies along with the victim. And your suffering continues after this life when you are reincarnated."

Those gathered renounced the killing of other beings. As a result, they were far better off in this life and in later rebirths.

The World of BUDDHISM

Karma is an important concept in several Eastern religions, especially Hinduism, Buddhism, and Jainism. At a basic level, karma is the law of cause and effect. Good actions produce good effects; evil actions produce evil effects. In the moral universe, thoughts, words, and deeds generate consequences that create the environment around each individual. This environment shapes the individual, by increasing or decreasing suffering.

Buddhist priests pray before a statue of Buddha at a monastery in Thailand. Buddhism is widely followed in the countries of Southeast Asia and East Asia, including China, Korea, Japan, and Vietnam.

The founder of Buddhism, Siddartha Gautama (563?-483? B.C.), was a prince who lived in northeastern India. Brought up in privilege, Siddartha eventually saw that there was much suffering in the world. He set out to overcome aging, sickness, and death. He gave up his former lifestyle and became an *ascetic* (wandering holy man). Eventually, Siddartha sat beneath a pipal tree and meditated until he reached a state known as Enlightenment, which was beyond human suffering. Siddartha's followers gave him the name Buddha, "the Awakened One."

Buddhist art uses symbols that can be identified by followers who might not be able to read. Endless knots suggest an endless cycle of cause and effect. Buddhists see the lotus (the white blossom toward the bottom of the illustration) as a symbol of Enlightment because it grows out of mud, through water, and into the light. In Buddhist teaching, mud represents the material world, water is experience, and sunshine is Enlightenment.

REINCARNATION

Reincarnation (REE ihn kahr NAY shuhn) is the belief that the soul survives after death and is reborn in the body of another person or some other living thing. In the religions of India, reincarnation is related to the law of karma. According to this law, a person's actions determine the type of body that the soul will enter during reincarnation. If a person leads a good life, his or her soul will be reborn in a higher state, such as the body of a priest. If a person leads a bad life, the soul will be reborn in a lower state, such as the body of a dog.

Rats drink milk left for them at a temple in India. Buddhists believe they should show loving-kindness to all forms of life, including animals. They also believe that it is wrong to hurt or kill animals.

HAINUWELE,
the Coconut Woman

The people of Seram Island use this story to explain the origin of the foods on which they rely as well as to explain why the gods no longer appear to them on Earth.

In the first days, nine families emerged from clusters of bananas growing on Seram Island. Among these ancestors of the Wemale (wee mayl) people was Ameta.

One day while hunting, Ameta spotted a boar and gave chase. As the boar ran, it slipped into a lake and drowned. When the boar's body washed ashore, Ameta found an object impaled on its tusk. He did not know that the object was a coconut, but he took it home. That night, in a dream, a spirit told him to plant the coconut. The next day, Ameta did so.

Six days later, a palm tree had grown. Ameta decided to cut some flowers to make tea. As he was climbing the tree, he cut his finger, and some blood dripped on one of the blossoms. Nine days later, he returned to the palm. He could not believe his eyes! A beautiful girl-child was growing where the blood-spotted blossom had been. Ameta cut her from the tree, wrapped her in leaves, and brought her to his house.

After only three days, the girl-child grew into a beautiful young woman. Ameta named her Hainuwele, or "Coconut

grew afraid. "This is not natural," they grumbled. So they dug a deep pit and threw Hainuwele in, burying her alive. Then the men danced on the mound until it was firmly packed.

When Hainuwele failed to come home, Ameta realized that she had been murdered. He dug up her body and cut her remains into pieces. He buried all the pieces, except for Hainuwele's arms. Soon, the buried pieces sprouted as plants no one had seen before. These were yams and other plants with thick roots that are good for food. These became the daily bread of the Seram Island people.

Ameta took Hainuwele's arms to the goddess Mulua Satene. The goddess was angry with the people. She created a dancing ground and drew a spiral at its center. From the woman's arms, Mulua Satene made a door. When all was ready, she called the dancers to her.

"Because you have taken life," she said, "I am leaving you today. Once I am gone, you may see me only after death. To see me, you will have to pass through this door." And then she vanished.

Woman." Hainuwele looked like an ordinary young woman, but she was not. When she relieved herself, she produced such precious objects as Chinese dishes, gongs, and jewels. Soon, Ameta grew very rich indeed.

One night, the people gathered for a festival. Hainuwele stood on the dancing ground and stunned them all by producing metal knives, golden earrings, and brass gongs. For nine days, she gave gifts to the dancers. No one had seen such wealth in one place. But the people

The World of
MOLUCCAS

Seram Island is part of the Moluccas (muh LUHK uhz), a group of Indonesian islands lying near the equator. The Moluccas were formerly known as the Spice Islands. It was spices from these islands that first attracted European traders to the Indonesian region.

GODS TO FOOD

The story of a deity who dies to become the *staple* (main) crop of a culture is widespread in myths. In the Americas, various peoples tell of murdered gods from whose bodies crops emerged. According to the Pueblo Indians, corn grows wherever the body of the murdered Corn Mother was dragged. In Maya myth, the Maker tried several ingredients to make people before finding that corn was the most suitable.

Bananas first grew in Southeast Asia, India, and parts of Australia.

← Coconuts are picked by men who climb up the bare tree trunks.

STAPLE FOODS

The coconuts and yams that feature in the story of Hainuwele are some of the most important food plants on Seram, along with other tuberous roots and bananas. Coconuts are not only eaten. The dried *kernel* (meat) of the coconut is also used to produce coconut oil, which is a major export for the island. The oil is used in foods and medicine and in some industrial processes. Coconut cake is also used as food for animals.

Seram is the largest island in the Moluccas. It is almost completely covered with dense forests.

Merchants and buyers meet in a traditional market (left) in the Moluccas, in an illustration from 1869. Archaeological evidence indicates that Seram Islanders traded with Chinese merchants at least 2,000 years ago. This long trading history may explain the mention of Chinese dishes and other ceramics in the myth of Hainuwele. Later, the islanders attracted European merchants because of their valuable spices.

THE SONS

Hindus tell this myth to explain the divine origins of the most important river in India, the Ganges, which waters the plains where Indian civilization emerged.

In ancient days, King Sagara (SAH guh ruh) had two wives but no children. The king and his wives found this misfortune intolerable, so they went to the mountains to pray to the gods to forgive their sins. At the end of a year, a great sage approached the king. "Ask a favor and it will be granted," this wise, holy man said. "Grant that my wives may bear children," replied the king. "So be it," the sage declared. "One wife will bear one son who will carry on your lineage. The other will bear 60,000 strong and famous sons." And so it happened. In time, Sagara's heir—the one son of his first wife—gave the king a grandson. He was called Amsumant, and he was kind and loved by the people.

One day, old King Sagara decided to sacrifice a horse that had been blessed by the gods. But the god Indra stole it. The king sent his 60,000 sons in search of it. "Dig up Earth league by league," he ordered, "until you have found the thief

OF SAGARA

and the Descent of the Ganges

and have returned the steed." Sagara's sons began digging. Eventually, in the underworld, the sons of Sagara discovered the sage Kapila (KAH pih luh) deep in meditation. Next to him was the sacrificial horse, nibbling grass. Mistaking the sage for the thief, the sons attacked him. The sage opened his eyes for the first time in years and said, "Hum." In an instant, the 60,000 sons of Sagara were reduced to ash.

When his sons did not return, Sagara sent his grandson, Amsumant, in search of them. He soon found the pile of ashes. He wept bitterly and wished to perform funeral rites but could find no water.

An ancestor appeared. "How shall their souls be carried to heaven if I do not purify their sins with water?" moaned Amsumant. The ancestor replied, "In heaven is Ganges (GAN jeez), daughter of Himalaya. She is the purifier of the world. Until her waters mingle with the ashes of these slain men, their souls will know no rest. Go and complete Sagara's sacrifice."

Amsumant took the horse and returned to his grandfather. He told him all he had heard. Sagara sacrificed the horse, but soon afterward he died. His kingdom

passed down over five generations to King Bhagiratha (buhg ee ruh thuh). Still no one had figured out how to bring Ganges to Earth.

Bhagiratha had no children. And so he ascended the Himalaya to live in severe simplicity. For 1,000 years, he kept his arms raised, ate only once a month, and controlled his five senses. Brahma (BRAH muh) the Creator was pleased. "Ask anything and it shall be granted," he said.

"O Grandfather of Worlds, grant that Ganges comes and mingles her waters with the ashes of my grandfathers so their souls may rest in peace." Brahma agreed, but he warned "Earth cannot withstand the force of Ganges's fall from heaven, so great are her waters."

Bhagiratha stood on the tip of one toe for a year, worshiping Shiva (SHEE vuh) the Destroyer. Only this god could bear the weight of Ganges's fall to Earth. At last, Shiva appeared. "I am pleased with you, O king. I will do as you ask and bear the daughter of Himalaya on my head." Ganges took a powerful form and plunged full force onto Shiva's head. Ganges could escape only little by little from Shiva's hair onto Mount Shankara and from there to Earth.

Bhagiratha descended the mountain in a chariot, and Holy Ganges followed behind. The king wound his way to the ocean and plunged into the hole to the underworld where the ashes of his ancestors still lay. Ganges followed, mingling her waters with their remains.

Brahma, Lord of All Worlds, spoke to the king, "You have at last fulfilled the vow of your fathers. Ganges will be your daughter and be called Bhagirathi (buhg ee ruh thee), and her purifying waters will remain on Earth hereafter to relieve all who bathe in her of their sin."

The World of
THE GANGES

The Ganges (GAN jeez), or Ganga, is the most sacred river in Hinduism. It begins in an ice cave 10,300 feet (3,139 meters) above sea level in the Himalaya mountains in northern India. The river then flows through Bangladesh, where it is known as the Padma. It runs 1,560 miles (2,510 kilometers) and empties into the Bay of Bengal.

The Kumbh Mela (KOOM muh lah) is one of the largest religious gathering on Earth. Over a month or so, some 100 million Hindus from India and around the world make a pilgrimage to perform rituals and to bathe in the Ganges. This is said to wash them clean of all their sins. The Kumbh Mela takes place every third year in one of four cities In India: Haridwar, Nasik, Allahabad (also known as Prayag), and Ujjain.

Millions of Indians enter the waters of the Ganges annually (above), cupping it in their hands and paying homage to their ancestors. During some ceremonies, worshipers float flowers and small clay boats filled with oil candles on the water (right). Commonly, devout Hindus travel great distances to mingle the ashes of their dead with the river's water.

Followers of the yoga school in the Hindu religion use yoga exercise to achieve their goal of isolation of the soul from the body and mind. They believe yoga exercise will help them gain an understanding of the meaning of their soul.

RISHIS

Indian myth features many *rishis* (sages), devout Hindus who try to perfect themselves through disciplines known as *yoga*. Through meditation, rishis eventually reach Enlightenment. They are frequently depicted as living in remote places. Disturbing a rishi while meditating can be dangerous, as Sagara's 60,000 sons discovered. Other times, sages provide blessings, counsel, or correction to those wishing to purify themselves.

THE FAIRY QUEEN of Mount Ophir

This story from Malaysia is a warning against allowing oneself to be driven by passion and greed. It also carries a lesson for rulers that they should not become too ambitious and self-centered.

In times gone by, Sultan Mansur (mahn SOOR) of Melaka gathered his counselors and told them, "We wish to marry a wife such as no man on Earth possesses."

"But, sir," replied his counselors, "You are already married to a Chinese princess and a Javanese princess."

"What of it?" demanded the Sultan. "Even rajas, who are not as powerful as I am, marry princesses. We desire to marry Puteri Gunung Ledang, the Fairy Queen of Mount Ophir (OH fuhr). No man has such a wife."

And so the king's guard was sent to the mountain. As they ascended, a great wind prevented the party from continuing. "Wait here!" Tun Mamat, the captain of the guard, said to his men, "I will climb up the mountain and present the Sultan's proposal."

Hand over hand, Tun Mamat and two other soldiers struggled up the mountain into the teeth of the wind. He and his men passed through a forest of singing bamboo until at last they reached a garden, near the place where the clouds touch the mountain.

In the garden, they saw four beautiful women. Tun Mamat greeted the women and explained his mission. "We are the Queen's guardians," the women said. "We will take your Sultan's proposal to her." And with that, they vanished.

Later that night, a woman, bent double with age, appeared to Tun Mamat and his men in the garden. "I bring the Queen's words," croaked the old woman. "If the Sultan of Melaka desires the hand of Puteri Gunung Ledang, he must build a bridge of gold and silver from his kingdom to the mountain. He must present as a betrothal gift seven trays filled with mosquito hearts, seven trays filled with the hearts of mites, a vat of water pressed from dried areca nuts, a vat of tears from virgins, and a cup of blood from Mansur's son."

Tun Mamat did not know it, but the old woman was none other than the Fairy Queen. She took on the appearance of a girl in the morning, a woman in the afternoon, and an old woman at night.

The captain of the guard returned with his party to Melaka and reported Puteri Gunung Ledang's demands to the Sultan. "All she requires, we can provide," said the Sultan when he heard them. "But we cannot give her the blood of our son for we would be beyond grief to take it from him."

But over time, madness possessed the Sultan. He simply had to marry Puteri Gunung Ledang. So he oppressed his people, squeezing them for every bit of gold and silver they possessed to build the required bridge. It was no difficult matter after that to gather the tears of many virgins, for his people were all extremely miserable.

When Puteri Gunung Ledang's gifts were almost completed, the Sultan turned his eyes toward his son.

"If we take the prince's blood, we can marry the Queen of the Mountain," he thought. It grieved the Sultan to consider this despicable act. But his desire for Puteri Gunung Ledang eventually won out.

One night, as his son was sleeping, the Sultan crept into his room with a dagger and a cup. Standing over the young man's bed, the Sultan raised his knife.

One thrust and the Queen would be his! Just as he started to deliver the blow, a hand caught his arm. It was Puteri Gunung Ledang herself! "Stop this madness!" she cried. "I could never marry a ruler who oppresses his people so cruelly and is capable of killing his own son!" Having saved the boy, Puteri Gunung Ledang vanished, returning to her mountain for good.

The World of THE FAIRY QUEEN

Malaysia (muh LAY zhuh or may LAY zhuh) is a country in Southeast Asia that is divided into two parts that lie about 400 miles (640 kilometers) apart, linked by the South China Sea. Malaysia's population is racially and ethnically diverse. Malays, Chinese, and Indians form the largest ethnic groups in the country.

A Malaysian couple wearing traditional clothing celebrates their wedding. Many stories with fairies are love stories in which young women are given choices and opportunities not commonly open to women in ancient cultures. They can, for example, choose their husband based on moral and personal qualities rather than being given to a man chosen by their father for political or economic reasons.

Shadow puppetry has been popular in Malaysia and other Southeast Asian countries for thousands of years. Puppet masters use delicate puppets cut from leather or paper to act out stories from myths and fairy tales.

THE UGLY WOMAN

The character of the ugly woman appears in many storytelling traditions. At the heart of the stories is a test of a suitor's worthiness. Often, a suitor is forced to marry the unattractive woman in exchange for something else he desires. If he proves worthy, she transforms into a beautiful woman. Other versions of the story, such as "The Fairy Queen of Mount Ophir," test the suitor's worthiness through an extravagant demand that reveals his true nature.

For centuries, Malaysia has been a meeting point of trade routes. The Malays and Indonesians built special ships called prahu (above) for sea trade. The ships could be sailed or rowed. Over time, many foreign merchants have been assimilated into Malay culture, together with foreign religions and ideas.

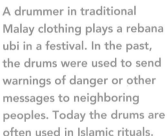

A drummer in traditional Malay clothing plays a rebana ubi in a festival. In the past, the drums were used to send warnings of danger or other messages to neighboring peoples. Today the drums are often used in Islamic rituals.

Although Malaysia has long been influenced by foreign customs, 18 tribes of Orang Asli, or "original people," still survive. These 150,000 individuals hunt and fish for food in the forests. The Orang Asli were traditionally animists, meaning they believed that objects and places had spirits. However, many have now adopted such *monotheistic* (single-god) religions as Islam and Christianity.

THE LEGEND OF

The people of Borneo tell this myth to explain the origins of two important geographical features—Lake Toba on the island of Sumatra, and Samosir Island that lies within the lake itself.

Once, a farmer named Toba worked a thin strip of land near a small lake. He was unmarried and childless. But he was content. Often, when the day's chores were done, he went fishing until dark. One evening, as he was fishing, he hauled a large golden fish from the water. He placed the fish in his basket and returned home.

"I will eat like a king," thought Toba, his mouth watering. But when he got home and opened the basket, he found that the fish was too beautiful to kill. So he decided instead to make it a pet. Toba put some water in a tub and carefully placed the fish inside it.

The next morning, the young man rose, fed the fish, and returned to his farm. When he arrived home that night, he found his house had been cleaned. Hot food waited on the table. "Who could have done this?" Toba wondered.

This went on for some days. Toba went to work in the morning and returned to a spotless house and food on the

LAKE TOBA

table. Curiosity overcame him. So one morning, Toba rose and got ready for work as usual. He walked out the door, but after taking a few paces, he quietly stole back to his house to see what he could see.

Through the window, Toba saw to his astonishment a beautiful young woman cleaning his dishes and straightening his house. Toba fell in love with the woman the moment he saw her. "Somehow, my fish has become a beautiful woman," he marveled.

Bursting through the door, Toba grabbed the young woman's arm before she could return to her fish form. "Please, won't you marry me?" Toba pleaded. At first the woman refused, saying "I only wish to repay you for sparing my life. It is my duty."

But at last, the beautiful woman relented. "I will marry you, Toba, but you must promise me one thing." "Anything! Name it!" "You must never reveal to another soul that I was once a fish," replied the woman. "If you can do that, I will be your wife."

Toba readily agreed. And so the couple lived together happily for many years.

The beautiful woman bore a beautiful daughter named Samosir (sah moh sihr). Growing up, the little girl worked with her mother in the house and played outside when her chores were done. Toba, of course, worked the farm. They were not rich, but they were happy.

One day, her mother said, "Samosir, please take your father his lunch. He will be starving by now."

So the girl took the basket with her father's lunch and set off down the hill toward the farm. But Samosir was hungry. She reached in the basket to nibble a little food. Still hungry, she reached into the basket again. By the

time she reached her father, the basket was empty.

Toba was famished. When he saw his daughter approaching with the lunch basket, he was delighted. But when he opened the basket and discovered it was empty, he flew into a rage. "What is this?" he shouted. "Where is my lunch?"

"I'm sorry, Papa, but I was hungry and could not resist. I ate your lunch," Samosir answered, tears gathering in her eyes. "You naughty little girl!" shouted Toba. "But what can you expect from the daughter of a fish?"

Samosir ran home crying. When her mother asked her what was wrong, the little girl was too upset to answer. At last, Samosir explained what she had done and how her father had called her the daughter of a fish.

Samosir's mother was horror-stricken. "Samosir, my love, you must leave this house immediately! Climb to the top of the mountain behind the house." "But, mother, why?" "Do as I say, girl!" her mother scolded. "If you don't, you will die!"

The little girl was so frightened she ran up the mountain as fast as she could go. Water poured from the house. Huge waves gushed forth. To Samosir's horror, the entire valley filled with water and surrounded the mountain where she watched helplessly. The mountain became an island. It is called Samosir Island to this day. As for the lake, it is called Lake Toba.

The World of
LAKE TOBA

Lake Toba is on the island of Sumatra in Indonesia. ➡
Both the lake and Samosir Island, which lies within the
lake, were created by a huge volcanic eruption about
75,000 years ago. The lake fills a *caldera* (craterlike
depression) left by the eruption. One of the largest
calderas known, the Toba caldera measures 20 by 60
miles (30 by 100 kilometers). Some scientists think that
the Toba eruption caused worldwide cooling that killed
off a large proportion of the human population.

The region around Lake Toba is home to the Toba
Batak, an *indigenous* (native) people of northern
Sumatra. The people are expert farmers, who grow
mainly rice.

FLOOD MYTHS

Flood myths are
universal in world cultures.
Often, the flood is sent by the
gods to punish human wrongdoing,
but this is not always the case. Water in
myths often symbolizes the chaos
preceding creation. It also symbolizes life
and birth. So flood myths involve a return
of the world to chaos in anticipation of a
rebirth. Usually, a hero works to
preserve a remnant
of the old world to help
in this rebirth.

The Toba Batak traditionally lived in communal
homes that housed four to six families. The boat-
shaped houses have three levels the Toba see as
symbolizing the three levels of the cosmos: the
underworld, middle world, and upper world. At
ground level, the space beneath the house was
used to keep animals. People used the middle
story for living and sleeping space. The upper
level, beneath the house's upswept roof ridge,
was used to store sacred family heirlooms.

LANDSCAPE IN MYTHOLOGY

Landscape plays a major role in mythology. Myths explain unusual natural features—why Crater Lake in the state of Oregon in the United States has a "hole in the top"; why a rock outcropping in Sipylus, Turkey, looks like a weeping woman; or why the stars in the Pleiades Cluster seem to be so closely packed together. Myths also associate certain land formations with the spirit-world. Indian tradition considers the sacred Ganges a goddess. Some Native American groups believe Mount Shasta in California is the home of spirits. Ancient Romans believed that Mount Etna, an active volcano in Sicily, rumbles and smolders because the god Zeus dropped the mountain on the fire-breathing monster Typhon.

Batak people of Samosir Island perform a traditional dance wearing native clothing.

DEITIES OF SOUTH ASIA AND SOUTHEAST ASIA

Asuras (ah SOO rahz)
In Hindu mythology, the asuras are demons who are perpetually at war with the gods.

Bhagiratha (buhg ee ruh thuh)
In Hindu mythology, Bhagiratha, the great-great-grandson of King Sagara, finally helped bring the holy river, the Ganges, to Earth.

Brahma (BRAH muh)
Brahma is the four-headed god who created the world. He is the first of the three gods in the Hindu *Trimurti* (trih MUR tee), or Trinity. It is believed that from his four heads came the four main Hindu holy books, the Vedas.

Brahman (BRAH muhn)
Brahman is the primeval substance in Hindu mythology, which is present in all things as the atman, the eternal soul; Brahman is represented on Earth by three gods, Brahma, Vishnu, and Shiva.

Dadhichi (DUH hee chee)
A Hindu sage, or wise person, who was one of Shiva's greatest worshipers, he gave up his bones to be used as weapons to defeat the demons and release the world's water for all living creatures.

Devas (DAY vahs)
For Hindus, the devas or suras are spirits who support the Trimurti, or Trinity. They are the half-brothers of the asuras, with whom they are constantly at war.

Devi
Devi, the partner of Shiva, is the most powerful of all Hindu goddesses. She is worshiped in two aspects: she is the benevolent mother of the world, but also fierce and terrible.

Dorje Gyatram (DAWR juh GY uh tram)
In Tibet, Dorje Gyatram, the Mighty Double Thunderbolt, created heaven and Earth with his scepter. He also made clouds, from which fell the first rain, forming the oceans.

Ganga (GAN uh)
For Hindus, the goddess Ganga is the personification of the sacred Ganges River, which flows through northern India.

Hainuwele
In Indonesia, a story tells how Hainuwele grew from a coconut tree but was murdered during a ritual dance. The goddess Mulua Satene avenged Hainuwele's death, turning some of her killers into the first animals by striking them with Hainuwele's arms.

Indra (IHN druh)

Indra is the thunder-god in Hindu texts and is the leader of the demigods (beings that are half human and half divine), conquering their enemies the asuras (demons).

Krishna (KRIHSH nuh)

Generally believed to be the eighth incarnation of the Hindu god Vishnu, Lord Krishna is the god of love and divine joy and protects the world from sorrow and evil.

Lac Long Quan (lak long won)

In Vietnamese myth, Lac Long Quan is the founder of the Vietnamese people. He married an immortal Chinese woman, Au Co, with whom he had a hundred sons from a hundred eggs; Quan's oldest son became the first king of Vietnam's Hung dynasty.

Mulua Satene

This goddess is the other half of Hainuwele, according to Indonesian folklore. She ruled over the first people who lived on Earth and was also ruler of the land of the dead.

Nagas (NAH guhz)

In Buddhist teaching, these are a race of snake- or dragonlike creatures, who can bestow both good and bad fates on men.

Puteri Gunung Ledang

In Borneo, the Sultan Mansur Ophir wanted to marry this fairy queen of Mount Ophir. She demanded a series of gifts, including a cup of his son's blood. But when the Sultan prepared to kill his son, she rejected him and disappeared.

Shiva (SHEE vuh)

The final Hindu god in the Trimurti, Shiva the Destroyer will one day bring fire to end our world, so that a new, better, and fairer world can be created.

Trimurti (trih MUR tee)

The Trimurti is the trinity of the chief Hindu gods, Brahma the Creator, Vishnu the Preserver, and Shiva the Destroyer.

Vishnu (VIHSH noo)

The second god in the Hindu Trimurti is Vishnu the Preserver, who looks after the present world that we live in. He is responsible for the restoration of the balance between good and evil in times of difficulty on Earth.

GLOSSARY

animists People who believe that all things in nature, including rocks, trees, rivers, or geographical locations, have their own spirits.

ascetic A person who leads a life of great self-denial to concentrate on spiritual fulfillment.

creation The process by which the universe was brought into being at the start of time.

creator In myth, a creator god is one who creates the universe or Earth, geographical features, and often all humans or a particular culture. Creation myths explain the origins of the world, but often do so by describing actions that seem to take place in a world that already exists.

demigod A lesser supernatural being; more than a human, less than a god; half human, half divine.

drought A prolonged period of unusually low rainfall that leads to a shortage of water.

dynasty A line of rulers who all come from the same family.

Enlightenment For Buddhists, the state in which people achieve freedom from the world of suffering and the cycle of birth, death, and rebirth.

karma In Buddhism and Hinduism, the sum of a person's good and bad actions, which decides his or her fate in future existences.

mantras Words or sounds that are repeated to aid meditation.

meditation The act of focusing the mind in order to achieve spiritual awareness.

monotheistic Describes a religion that has a single god.

myth A traditional story that a people tell to explain their own origins or the origins of natural and social facts and happenings. Myths often involve gods, spirits, and other supernatural beings.

naga A mythical, dragonlike creature with the body of a snake but often the head of a human.

reincarnation The rebirth of a soul in another body after death.

ritual A solemn religious ceremony in which a set of actions are peformed in a specific order.

sacred Something that is connected with the gods or goddesses and so should be treated with respectful worship.

sacrifice An offering made to a god or gods, often in the form of an animal or even a person who is killed for the purpose. Sacrifices also take the shape of valued possessions that might be buried, placed in caves, or thrown into a lake for the gods.

sage Someone who is famed for his or her profound wisdom.

shaman A person who enters a trance during a religious ritual to gain access to the world of the spirits; in many cultures, a shaman is seen as a link between humans and the spiritual world.

supernatural Describes something that cannot be explained by science or by the laws of nature, which is therefore said to be caused by such beings as gods, spirits, or ghosts.

Vedas Four collections of texts that form the earliest basis of Hindu beliefs. They were composed between 1500 and 700 B.C.

yoga A practice involving specific postures and controlled breathing to achieve spiritual awareness.

FOR FURTHER INFORMATION

Books

Claus, Peter, and Sarah Diamond (eds.). *South Asian Folklore: An Encyclopedia.* Routledge, 2003.

Clements, William M. (ed.). *The Greenwood Encyclopedia of World Folklore and Folklife: Volume 2: Southeast Asia and India, Central and East Asia, Middle East.* Greenwood, 2006.

Coomaraswamy, Ananda K., and Sister Nivedita. *Myths of the Hindus and Buddhists* (Dover Books on Anthropology and Ethnology). Dover Publications, 1967.

Cotterell, Arthur, and Rachel Storm. *The Ultimate Encyclopedia of Mythology.* Southwater, 2012.

Hayes, Amy (ed.). *Beliefs, Ritualism and Symbols of India* (Man, Myth, and Magic). Cavendish Square Publishing, 2014.

Korom, Frank J. *South Asian Folklore: A Handbook.* Greenwood, 2006.

Leeming, David, *A Dictionary of Asian Mythology.* Oxford University Press, 2001.

Mackay, Jenny. *Hindu Mythology* (Mythology and Culture Worldwide). Lucent Books, 2015.

National Geographic Essential Visual History of World Mythology. National Geographic Society, 2008.

Pattanaik, Devdutt. *Indian Mythology: Tales, Symbols, and Rituals from the Heart of the Subcontinent.* Inner Traditions, 2003.

Pattanaik, Devdutt. *Myth = Mithya: A Handbook of Hindu Mythology.* Penguin India, 2008.

Philip, Neil. *Eyewitness Mythology* (DK Eyewitness Books). DK Publishing, 2011.

Phillips, Charles, Michael Kerrigan, and David Gould. *Ancient Indian Myths and Beliefs* (World Mythologies). Rosen, 2012.

Schomp, Virginia. *Ancient India* (Myths of the World). Marshall Cavendish Benchmark, 2010.

Williams, George M. *Handbook of Hindu Mythology* (Handbooks of World Mythology). Oxford University Press, 2008.

Websites

http://www.godchecker.com/pantheon/indian-mythology.php
A directory of subcontinent deities from God Checker, written in a light-hearted style but with accurate information.

http://www.godchecker.com/pantheon/south-east-asian-mythology.php
The God Checker index of deities from Southeast Asia, with links to individual entries.

http://www.godchecker.com/pantheon/tibetan-mythology.php
The God Checker list of Tibetan gods.

http://www.pantheon.org/areas/mythology/asia/hindu/articles.html
Encyclopedia Mythica page with an essay on Indian mythology and links to many pages about deities.

http://www.mythome.org/Indian.html
A page with an exploration of Indian mythology and links to creation and flood myths.

http://www.crystalinks.com/india.html
This Crystal Links page has links to articles about all aspects of ancient Indian history and mythology.

INDEX

PRONUNCIATION KEY

Sound	As in
a	hat, map
ah	father, far
ai	care, air
aw	order
aw	all
ay	age, face
ch	child, much
ee	equal, see
ee	machine, city
eh	let, best
ih	it, pin, hymn
k	coat, look
o	hot, rock
oh	open, go
oh	grow, tableau
oo	rule, move, food
ow	house, out
oy	oil, voice
s	say, nice
sh	she, abolition
u	full, put
u	wood
uh	cup, butter
uh	flood
uh	about, ameba
uh	taken, purple
uh	pencil
uh	lemon
uh	circus
uh	labyrinth
uh	curtain
uh	Egyptian
uh	section
uh	fabulous
ur	term, learn, sir, work
y	icon, ice, five
yoo	music
zh	pleasure